This edition published in 1994 by
SMITHMARK Publishers Inc.
16 East 32nd Street
New York, NY 10016

SMITHMARK books are available for bulk purchase,
for sales promotion and premium use. For details
write or call the manager of special sales,
SMITHMARK Publishers Inc., 16 East 32nd Street,
New York, NY 10016; (212) 532–6600.

© 1994 Anness Publishing Limited
Boundary Row Studios
1 Boundary Row
London SE1 8HP

Reprinted 1996

ISBN 0-8317-0886-7

Editorial Director Joanna Lorenz
Editorial Consultant Jackie Fortey
Designer Joy Fitzsimmons

Typeset by MC Typeset Limited
Printed and bound in China

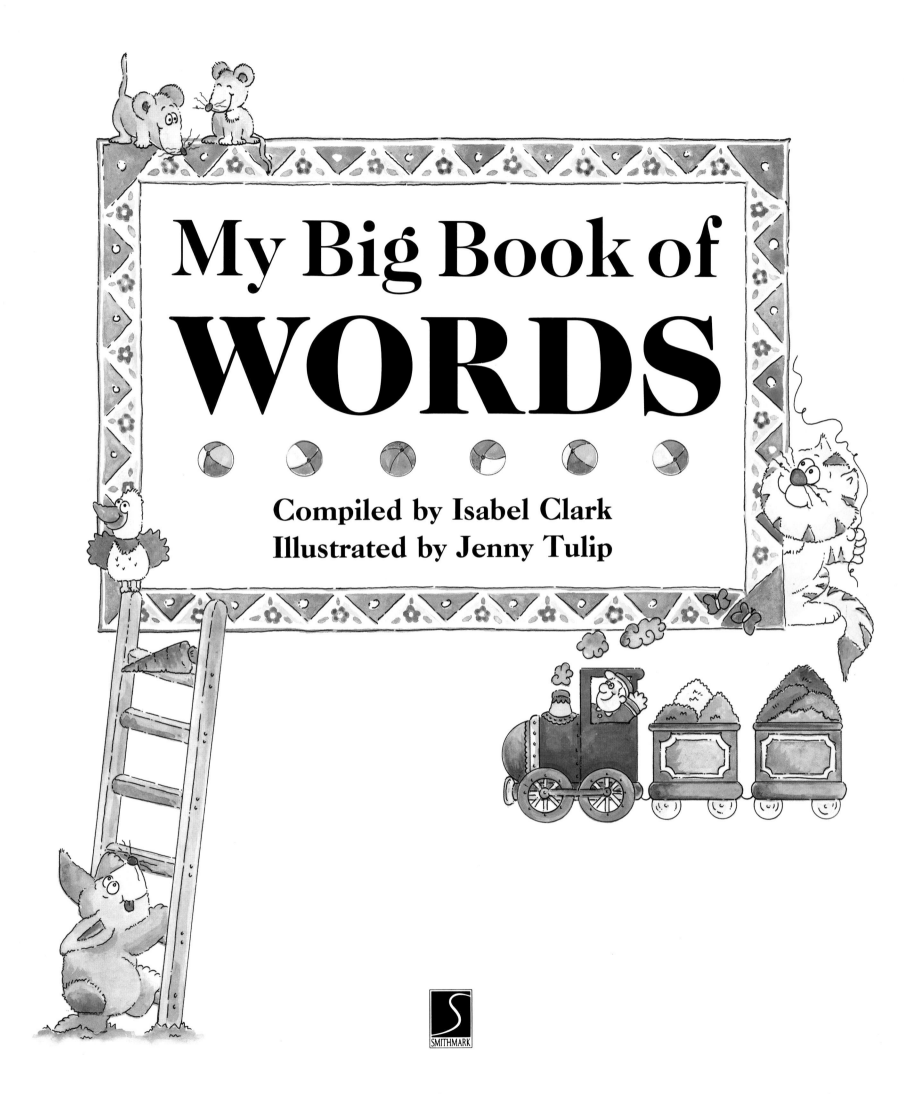

My Big Book of
WORDS

Compiled by Isabel Clark
Illustrated by Jenny Tulip

SMITHMARK

CONTENTS

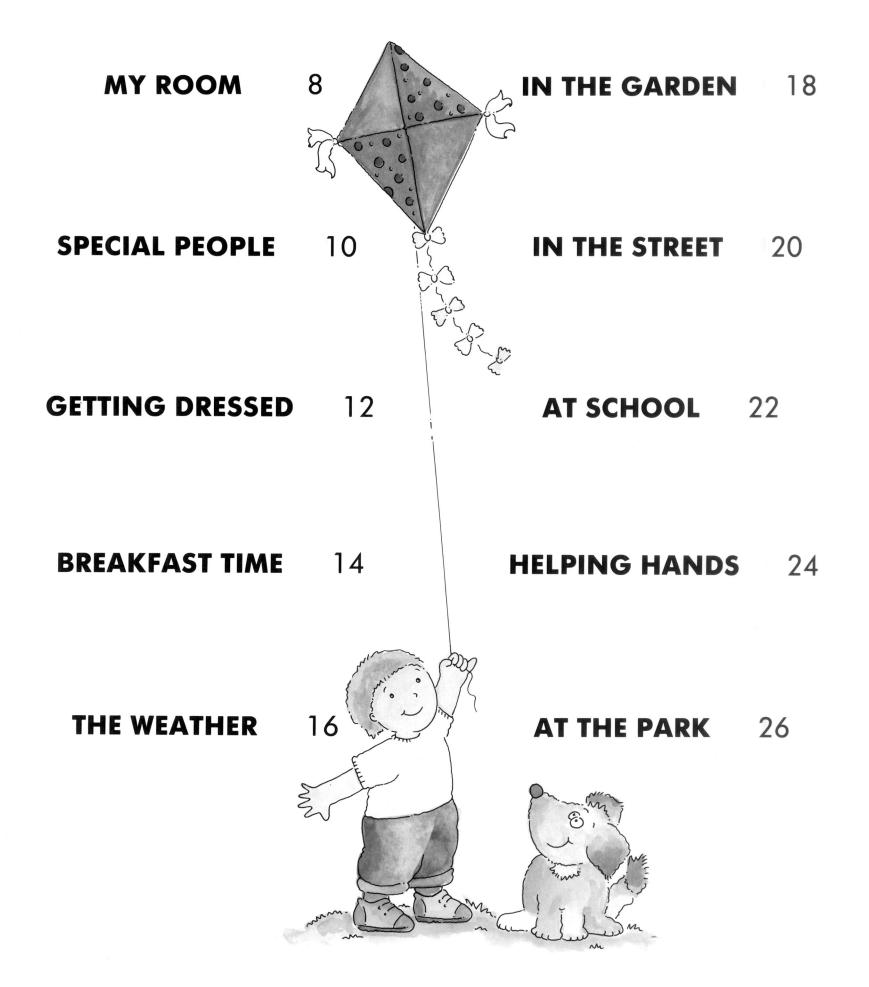

CONTENTS

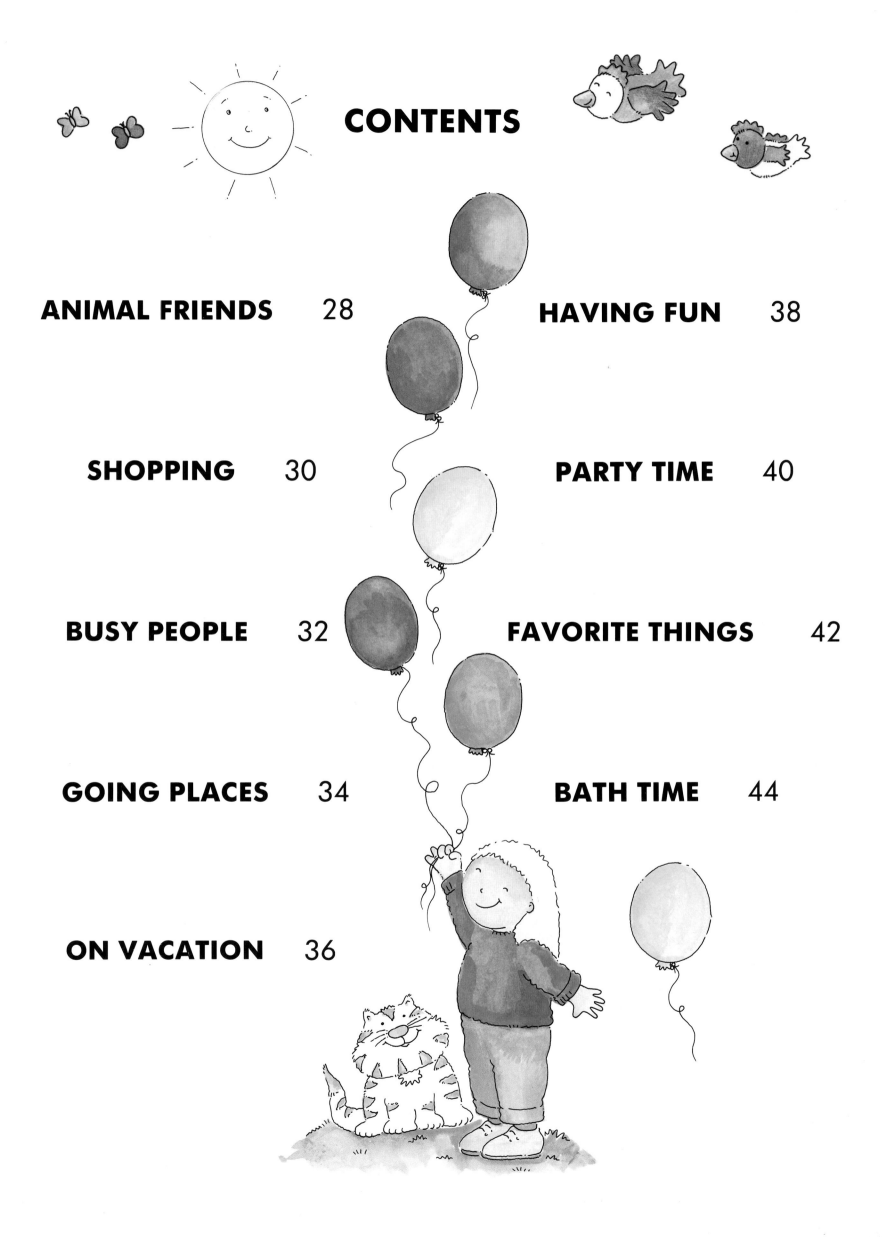

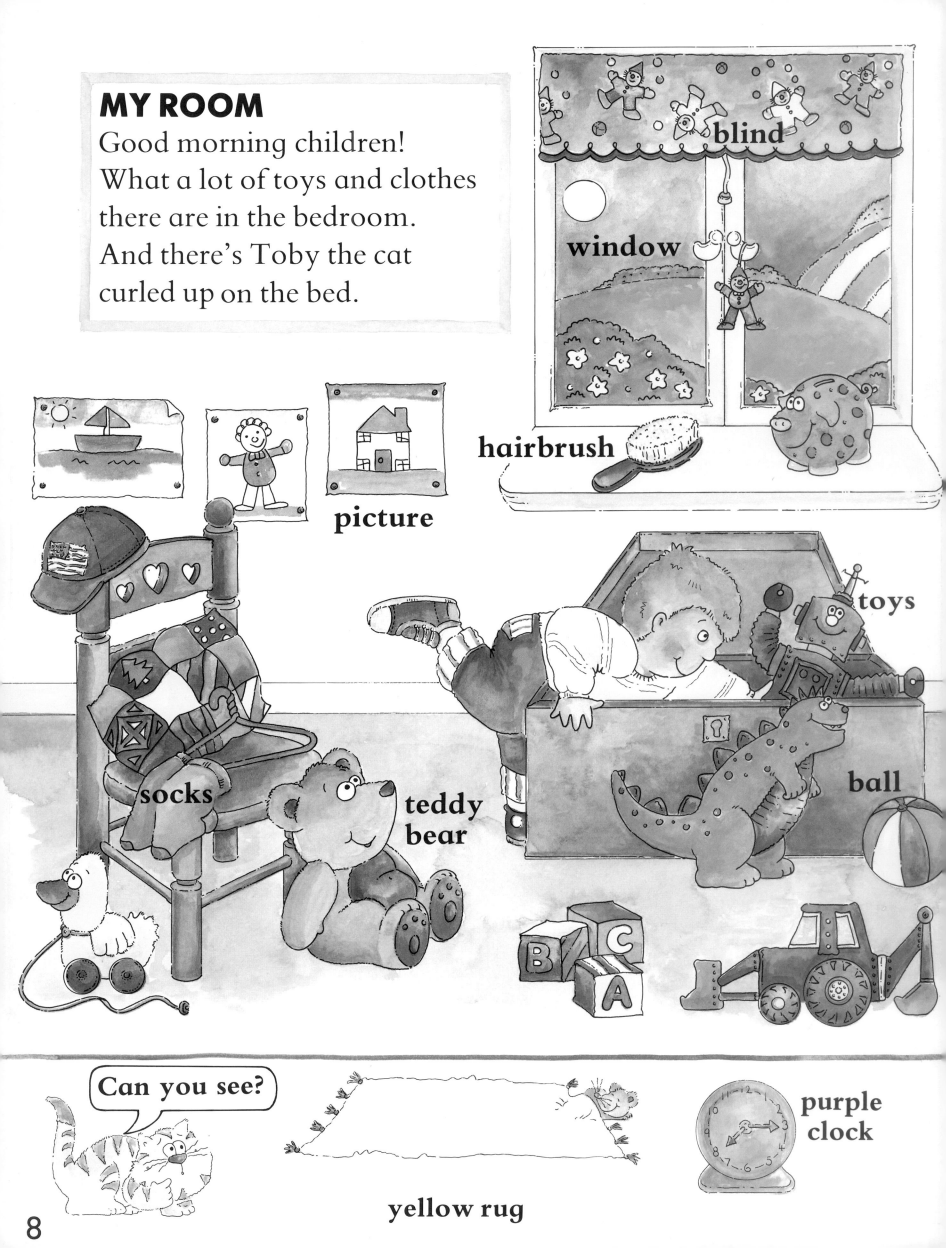

MY ROOM

Good morning children!
What a lot of toys and clothes
there are in the bedroom.
And there's Toby the cat
curled up on the bed.

blind

window

hairbrush

picture

socks

teddy bear

toys

ball

Can you see?

yellow rug

purple clock

8

mobile

bookshelf

clock

comb

cupboard

quilt

bed

pillow

cat

rug

clothes

slippers

pair of slippers

brown teddy bear

green socks

9

SPECIAL PEOPLE

Family and friends are special people. It is good to see them when they come to visit. Mom and a neighbor are talking. What is the matter with the dog?

boy

Dad

razor

sponge

baby

computer

cousin

brother

sister

crayons

Can you see?

Grandpa sleeping

dog growling

Grandpa

bird cage

knitting

cane

bag

Grandma

wool

neighbor

Mom

iron

postman

dog

baby laughing

Mom talking

Dad shaving

11

GETTING DRESSED

It is time to get dressed. What clothes are the children going to wear today? Baby needs someone to help him put all his clothes on.

scarf

skirt

sweater

undershirt

chest-of-drawers

pocket

socks

jacket

jeans

diaper

underwear

Can you find?

polka-dotted T-shirt

yellow sweater

12

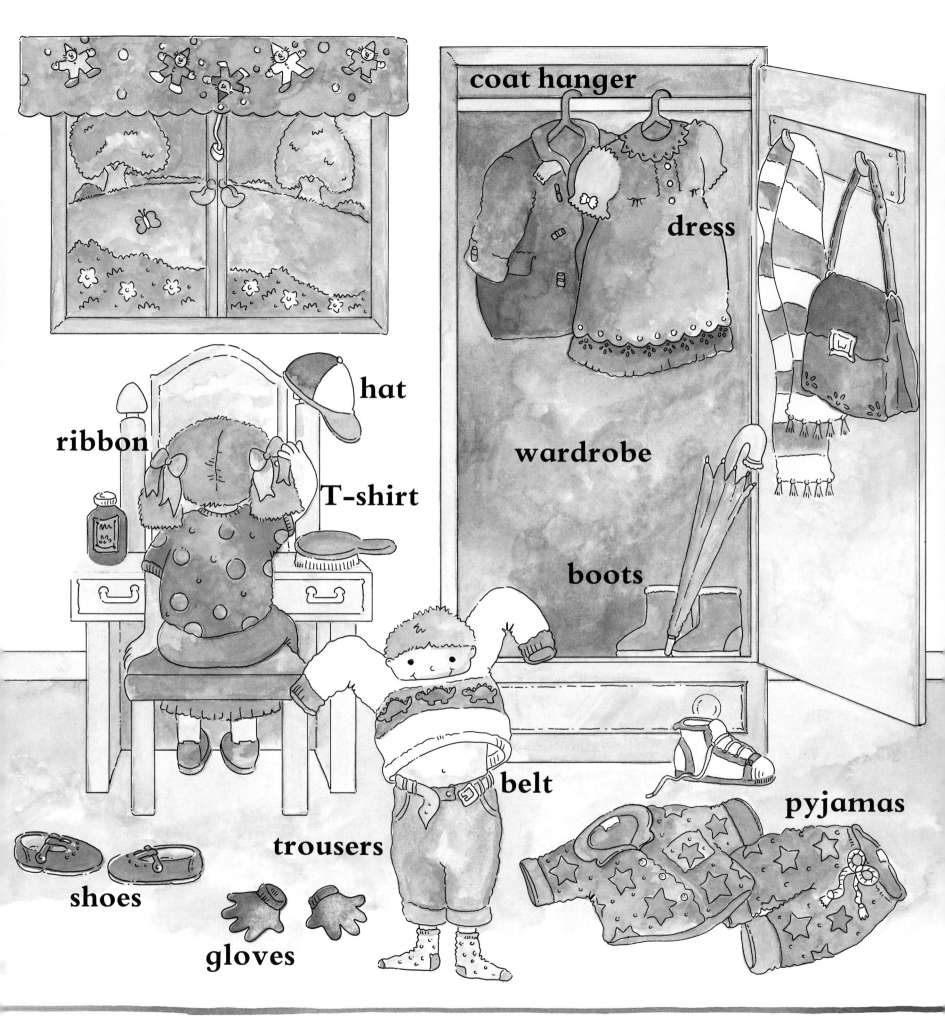

coat hanger

dress

ribbon

hat

T-shirt

wardrobe

boots

belt

pyjamas

trousers

shoes

gloves

blue jeans

red shoes

green jacket

13

BREAKFAST TIME

At breakfast time everyone is hungry and wants something to eat. Mom is busy cooking. Who is going to get the big pancake?

jar

electric teapot

toaster

pitcher

cereal

spoon

egg

cereal box

jam

mug

highchair

lunchbox

apple

knife

fork

Can you see?

green apple

bowl of cereal

14

pasta jar

pancake

frying pan

bread

refrigerator

apron

stove

bread board

oven

dog bowl

celery

basket

tomato

carrot

boiled egg

big pancake

dog bowl

15

THE WEATHER

What is the weather like today? It is hot and sunny down by the river but the wind is blowing and black clouds are coming over the hill.

sun

windmill

river

boy

bulrushes

sun hat

bread

girl

picnic basket

sunglasses

Can you see?

bright sun

black clouds

16

rainbow

cloud

hill

leaves

tree

umbrella

raindrops

snowflakes

girl

raincoat

puddle

boots

snowman

sled

steppingstones

raindrops falling

picnic basket

windmill

17

IN THE GARDEN

It is great to play outside in the garden. Friends come along and help to build a sand castle. Look at all the birds. What are they doing?

nest

wall

swing

sandbox   sandcastle

bush

birdbath

wheelbarrow

snail

watering can

Can you see?

lawn mower

birdbath

18

gate

shed

spade

hose

flowerpot

garden chair

flowers

worms

lawn

lawn mower

snail

worms

flowerpot

19

IN THE STREET

There are all kinds of shops and houses along the street. Some of the people have been busy shopping. What have they bought?

traffic lights

house

front door

pedestrian

wheel

car

bread

road

dog

sidewalk

Can you see?

green car

cyclist

20

chimney

tv aerial

roof

clock

store

safety helmet

cyclist

mail box

bicycle

curb

dog leash

shopping basket

clock

traffic lights

safety helmet

21

AT SCHOOL

It is fun to be at school and everybody enjoys listening to the teacher when it is story time. Where do the children hang their coats?

A B C D E F G H

blackboard

painting

teacher

school bell

chalk

desk

bookshelf

book

paper

pencils

Can you find?

building bricks

paint box

school bus

globe

scissors

crayons

bookbag

paint box

chair

paintbrush

coat

playhouse

table

lunchbox

building blocks

book

school bell

pencils

23

HELPING HANDS

There are all sorts of ways to be helpful. It is good when we can help our friends. Let's look for people whose job it is to help others.

library

librarian

overalls

garbage cart

garbage collector

broom

litter

policewoman

Can you see?

doctor

policewoman

24

doctor

stethoscope

bandages

sling

uniform

nurse

wheelchair

garbage can

guide-dog

harness

helmet

nozzle

fireman

walking-stick

hose

hospital

librarian

fireman

guide-dog

AT THE PARK

There are no cars in the park so children can run about. They can play with their friends on the swings and slide. Where can they buy ice cream?

swings

bulletin board

town map

grass

jump rope

skateboard

Can you see?

bulletin board

slide

tree

weathervane

fence

ice cream
stand

garbage
can

bench

slide

balloon

ball

stroller

pond   fish

ducks

ducklings

swings

skateboard

ducks

27

ANIMAL FRIENDS

Here are some of our animal friends out in the countryside. The farmer keeps his animals in fields. The other animals live in the Safari Park.

pigeon

spider

squirrel

sheep

horse

lamb

foal

cow

rabbit

calf

farmer

frog

duck

fish

mouse

Can you find?

sheep

zebra

bird

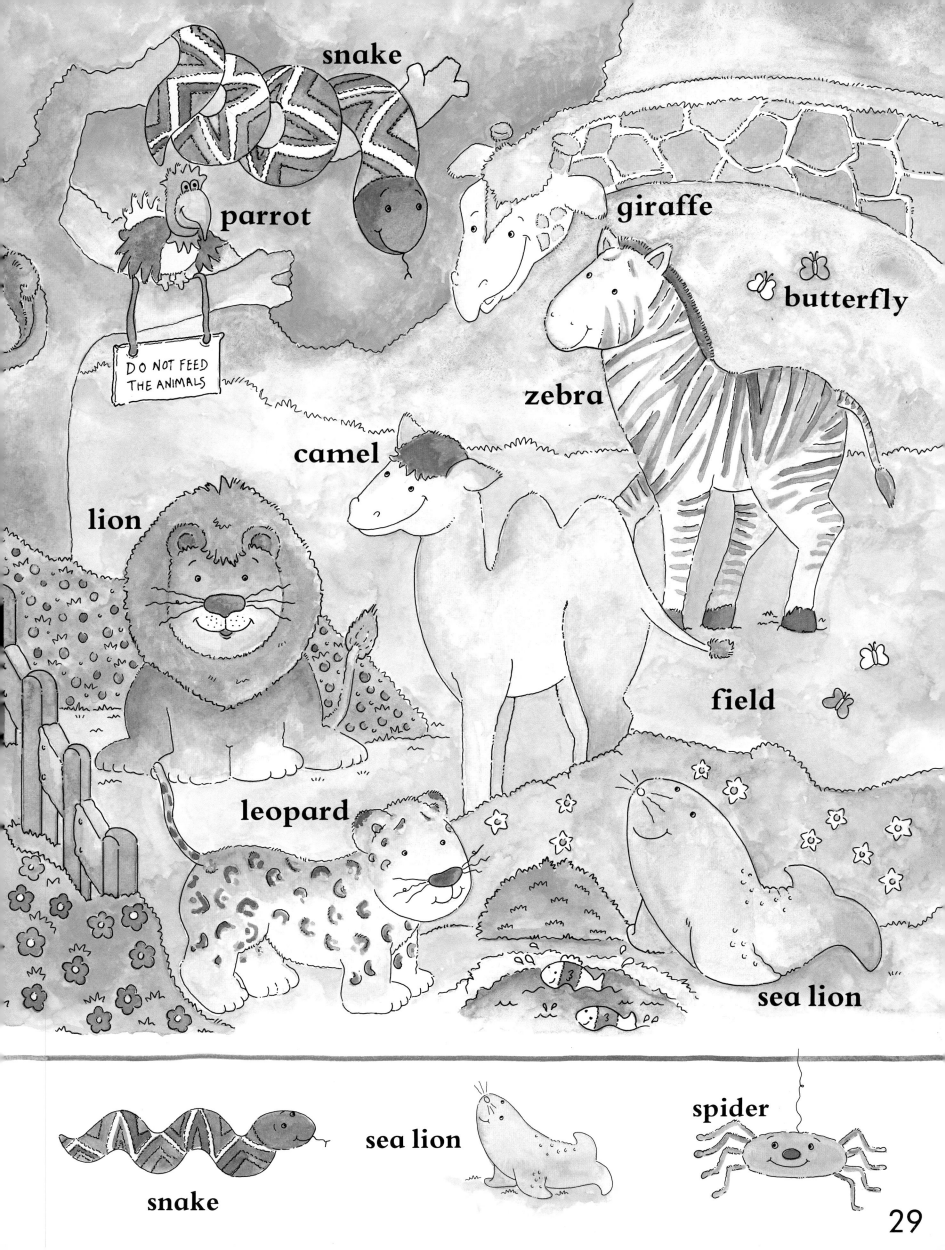

snake

parrot

giraffe

butterfly

zebra

camel

lion

field

leopard

sea lion

DO NOT FEED THE ANIMALS

snake

sea lion

spider

SHOPPING

All the family help with the shopping. They visit the big supermarket and choose things from the shelves. Who has the big box of food?

lemons

grapes

bananas

apples

shopping cart

customer

money

purse

can

eggs

shopping list

basket

Can you see?

bread

shopping list

30

milk

juice

bread

cheese

bottle

cashier

man

register

check-out

carrot

box

shopping bag

cheese

shopping cart

register

31

BUSY PEOPLE

Men and women go to work and do lots of different jobs. Some people work indoors, while others work outside. What do you call a person who fixes cars?

crane

jogger

safety helmet

carpenter

cement mixer

builder

bricklayer

ladder

microphone

pliers

saw

bricks

tool bag

tv reporter

Can you see?

bricklayer

builder

32

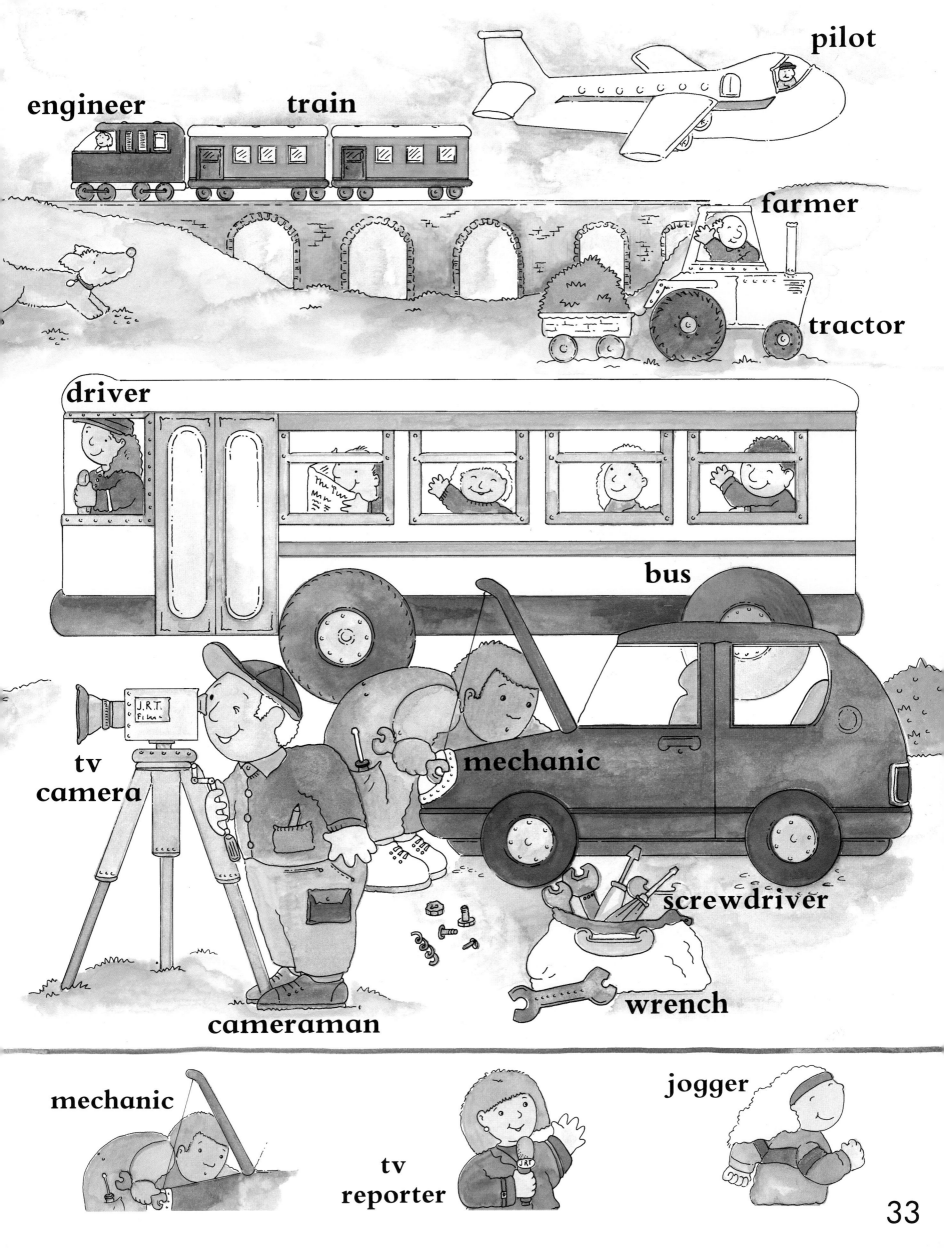

pilot

engineer

train

farmer

tractor

driver

bus

tv camera

mechanic

screwdriver

cameraman

wrench

mechanic

tv reporter

jogger

33

GOING PLACES

There are all sorts of ways to travel. People can ride in a car, a train, a bus, a boat, a truck or a plane. How would you like to travel?

parachute

ship

truck

wheel

car

motorcycle

Can you see?

motorcycle

truck

34

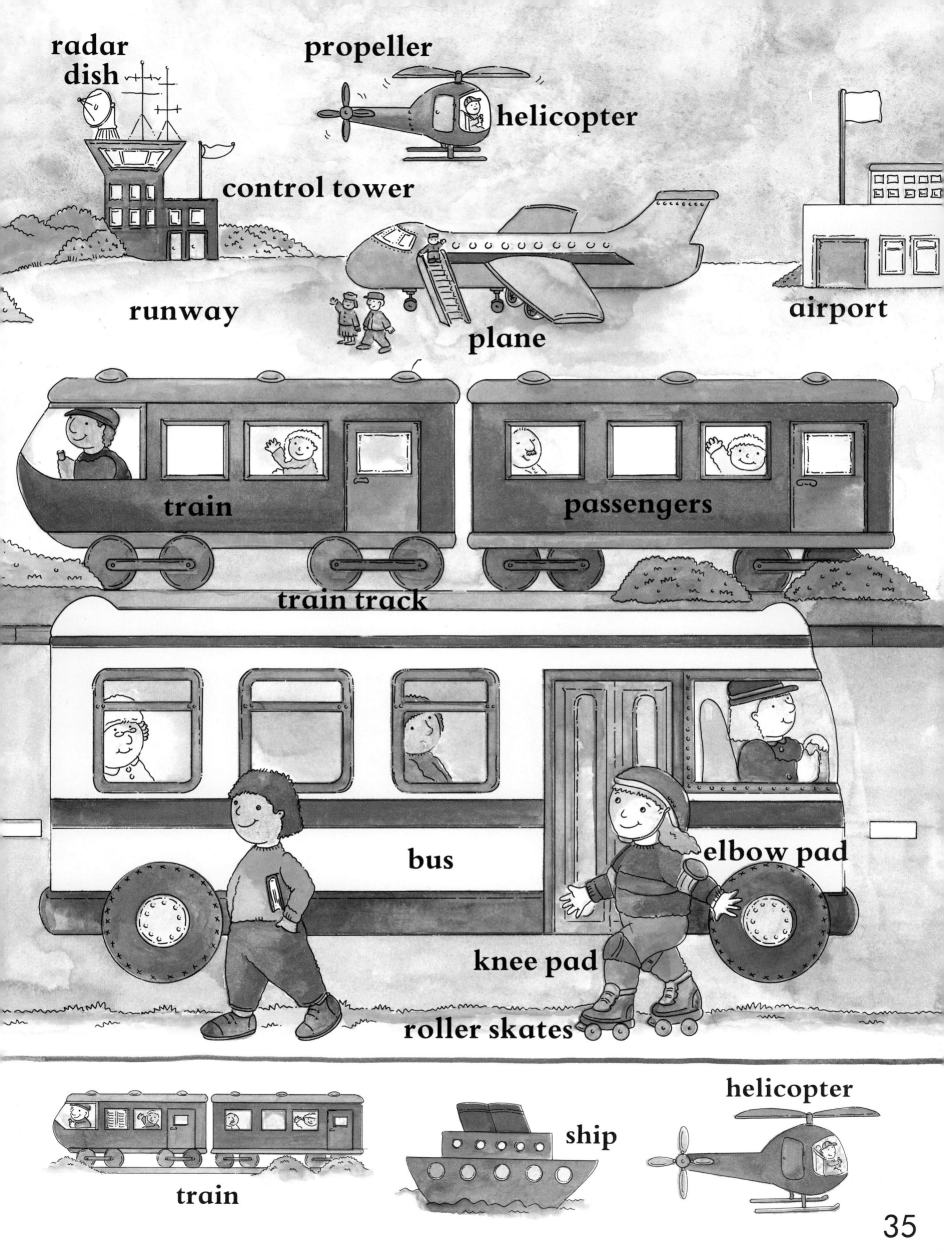

radar dish

propeller

helicopter

control tower

runway

plane

airport

train

passengers

train track

bus

elbow pad

knee pad

roller skates

train

ship

helicopter

35

ON VACATION

It is lovely to go away on vacation. There are different places to explore and exciting things to do with new friends. How are the people going to get down to the beach?

flag

hotel

fence

sea gull

umbrella

sand

ice cream

swimsuit

sandcastle

towel

lounge chair

starfish

shell

beach

Can you see?

umbrella

steps

36

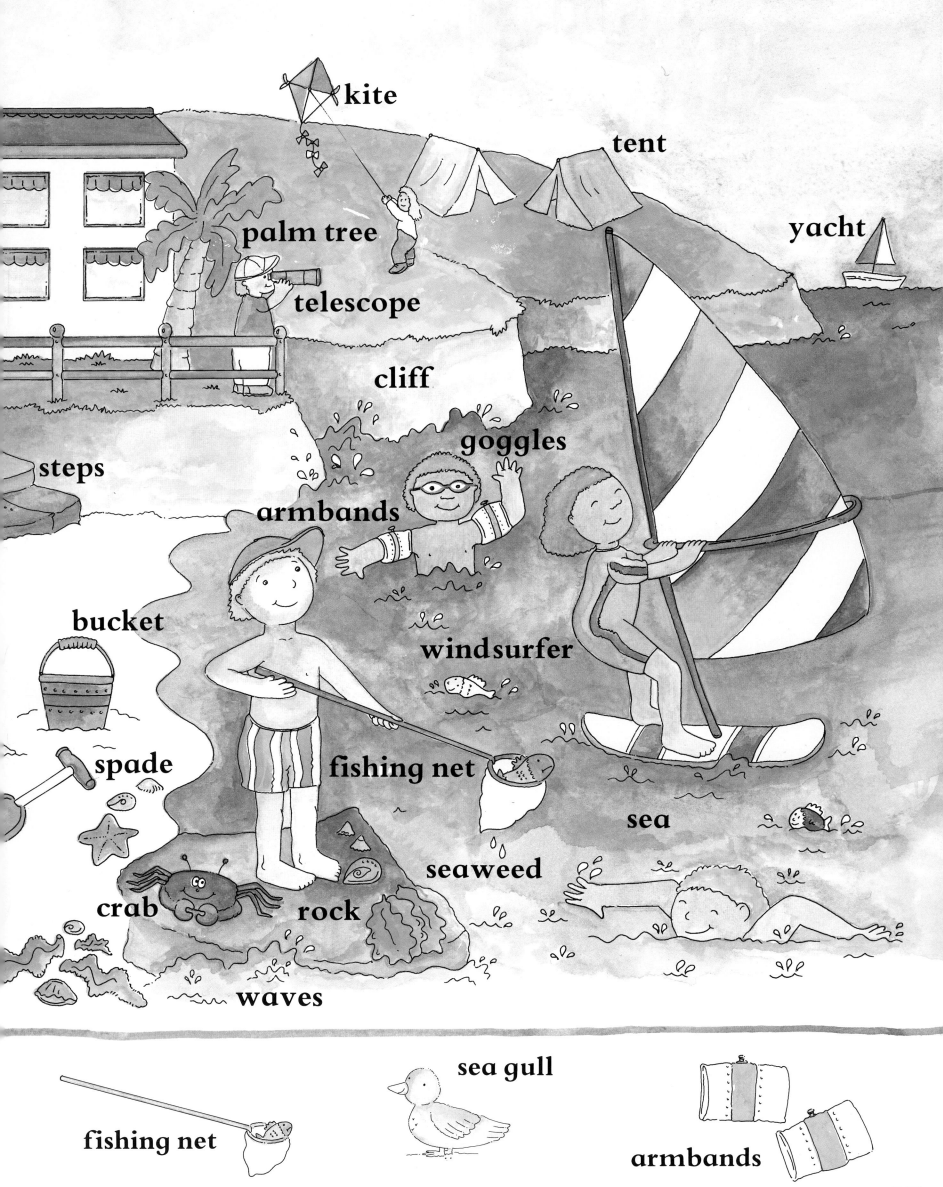

kite

tent

yacht

palm tree

telescope

cliff

goggles

steps

armbands

bucket

windsurfer

spade

fishing net

sea

crab

seaweed

rock

waves

fishing net

sea gull

armbands

HAVING FUN

Sometimes we have to work hard, but the best times are when we can have fun. Here are games people play. Which do you like best?

kite

frisbee

helmet

shield

teddy

cloak

tricycle

bopper hopper

toy cat

roller skates

Can you see?

jump rope

teddy

38

goal

soccer ball

helmet

baseball bat

swimsuit

rubber ring

skateboard

jump rope

tennis racket

tennis ball

tennis racket

toy cat

frisbee

PARTY TIME

Someone is having a birthday party. Can you see who it is? Friends bring presents, play games and everyone has lots of good things to eat.

tape recorder

clock

balloon

bookshelf

donkey

blindfold

tail

dog

wrapping paper

Can you find?

candles

birthday cake

40

party hat

candles

birthday cake

birthday card

straws

pitcher

jelly

plate

cookies

jigsaw puzzle

presents

sandwiches

jigsaw puzzle

birthday card

donkey

41

FAVORITE THINGS

We all have things which are special to us. They make us feel good and we like to share them with our friends. What are your favorite things?

dog

puppy

rabbit

fishing rod

fishing hat

Grandma

Grandpa

butterfly

candy

flowers

Can you see?

train set

fishing rod

42

ice cream

best friend

Dad

Mom

balloon

cat

family

snowflakes

scarf

coat

snowman

train set

photo album

photographs

Grandpa

balloon

dog

candy

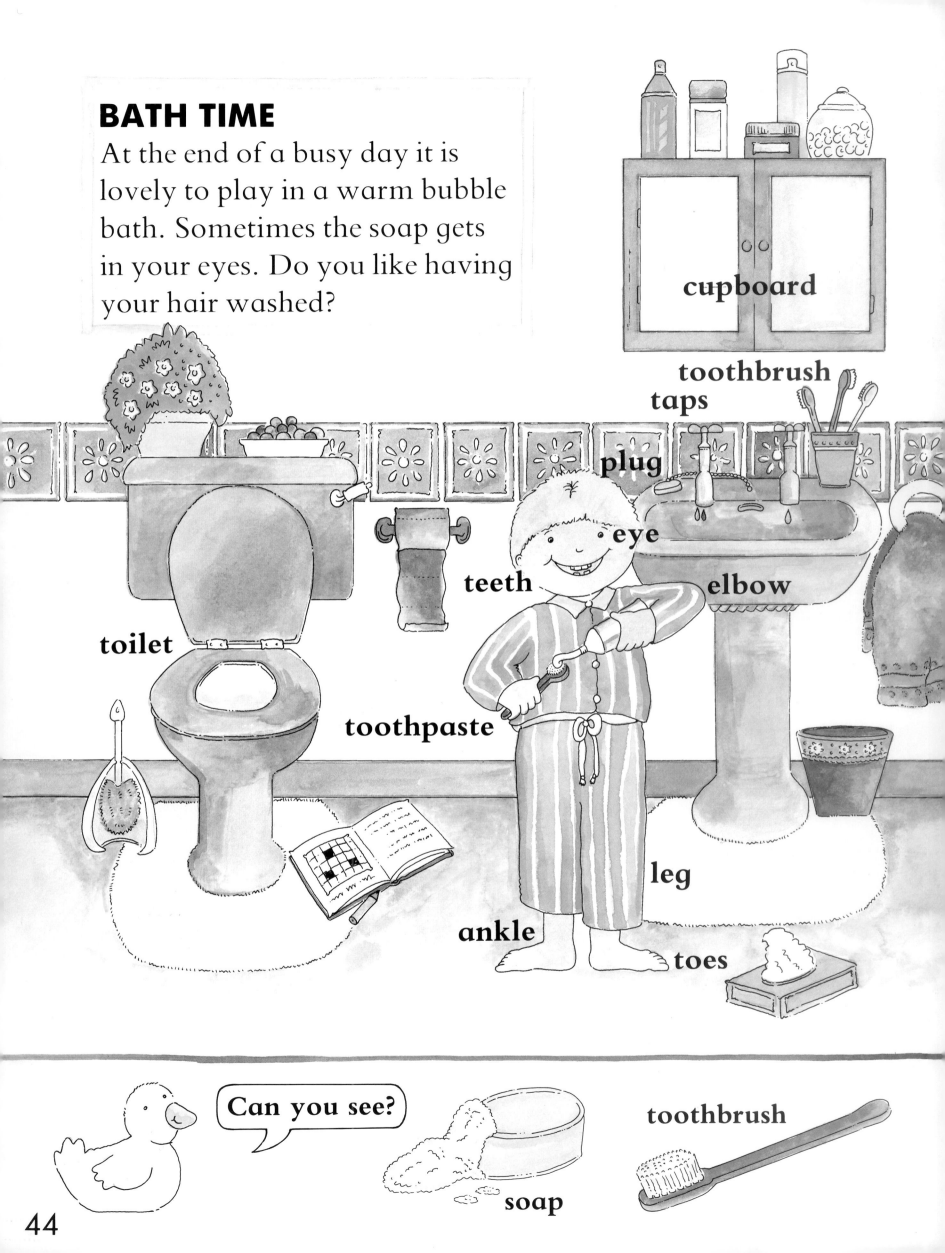

BATH TIME

At the end of a busy day it is lovely to play in a warm bubble bath. Sometimes the soap gets in your eyes. Do you like having your hair washed?

cupboard

toothbrush

taps

plug

eye

teeth

elbow

toilet

toothpaste

leg

ankle

toes

Can you see?

soap

toothbrush

dressing gown

shower

bubbles

finger

ear

neck

face

hair

nose

bath toy

towel rack

water

washcloth

bath

mouth

shower cap

soap

arm

hand

boat

towel

bathmat

foot

bath toy

boat

shower